2132

THE END OF MAN

The time has come for humanity to end
The time has come
The time has come

Yes time will tell (Bob Marley)
Many of us think we are living in heaven but
you're living in hell.

The time has come
The time has come
Humanity will pay – must pay

No more free ride
No more lies
No more deceit

No more greed
No more war
The life of man – humanity will be no more

She did reach the top of the mountain hence
truly woe be unto man – humanity.

Kaboom
Kaboom
Kaboom

Man played the ultimate game
The wars of the world
Different lands

Now time tells
Reveal

Woe be unto humanity when death truly comes
Woe be unto the children of man
Woe be unto you because hell comes
Hell is almost here

Many will weep because they did sin
Acted like the fool
We did sin for death and now we must literally
die with death – pay.

Michelle Jean

In all I see I see the end of man – humanity
I see the wars
The killings
The deceit and woe be unto America – the lands of earth.

I see the guns of old
I see the war of old and nothing lived
No one was saved
Hence I say woe be unto America and humanity come 2014 and beyond because that land is doomed; never to rise again.

The war that I see makes gun play in the Okay Carrel look like child's play because it is that fierce and deadly.

No life is safe – not even the ripe tomatoes because they did become spoiled, hence humanity cannot cry because this is their own doing – will – evil will. All I am seeing now is war not rumours of war but war itself – death.

Everything is winding down hence the end of man – humanity is here.

Woe be unto America because they will not escape the judgement. Many will die because they did kill, seek to kill; participated in a war including wars they knew nothing about.

This is there destruction because nothing will or can save them now.

The war is here for them and truly woe be unto that land because they are going to be utterly destroyed thus saith the Lord thy God meaning it is so.

France and Canada you are duly warned because Iran is going to come into play with your land and you are being warned against them.

Do not get involved with them because their president is a liar and all they do is based on lies.

Islam will come into play in all of this because the Babylonians will take the stage with their religious lies and you cannot fall prey to the council of the dead like many black people do.

They are a race that do not listen hence they follow the Babylonians – Islamic Way to their deaths – hell. Hence HELL IS FULL OF BLACK PEOPLE AND RECRUITING MORE.

White people it is time to stop the fighting – war. It's time to stop the killing because in truth none of you know what you are fighting for. From the beginning until now you have been fighting and I still cannot see what you – your race is fighting for.

You cannot tell someone or another nation that they are cursed when your race is the cursed race. Your race was the race that got cursed and or a spell was cast upon you and you have to break that spell.

If you were to go back to the book of sin Noah cursed Canaan, but it was not Noah that cursed you it was a woman and I've already told you this.

The black race is not the cursed race. They are just stiff necked and stubborn; very disobedient because we lack the patience for certain things.

I will not go over this again because I've already told you this before.

I've also told you who received the mark of the beast and who has it.

I've told you what Satan looks like and I've told you what hell fire looks like.

The end of man – humanity is winding down hence many will not live to see 2032.

Yes many of you are gearing up for this new world order but sins time is up now. The harvest comes and every man woman and child must pay according to his or her work.

This harvest is going to brutal hence many lands are going to lose it all. Food and water is going to become scarce hence the devil's people will not have a home or a leg to stand on.

Billionaires will lose it all because their debts that they have to pay Satan no not Satan but Melchesidec cannot be repaid. They have their DDC hence they fall under the Abrahamic Code of law and conduct - Death.

Many have killed to maintain their stay with sin hence their place is with death and none other.

As for their children, the same goes for them. Death has them hence there can be no resurrection of the dead or for the dead.

As 2013 comes to a close many things will start happening and as I see them I will let you know. Many things I cannot see but know for a surety The United States of America will never be the same. Like I said, this old war of people dying is a new war that is coming and woe be unto the land. I keep seeing America, the fighting hence 2014 will be a devastating year for them. All I see for them is war and death. I told you I did see the Washington Monument falling hard. Hence how the mighty has fallen. Babylon has and will fall and fall harder and harsher than any other nation because they did sell out their own and left the land indebted to sin – Satan as you call him.

Their national debt is a monumental sin that cannot be repaid, hence the fall of Babylon (America) will affect the global market place – world.

I will not get into the European Market Place because they too are going to feel it especially Germany and England. Do not quote me on the Germany and England because I have not seen their destruction but I know for a fact Scotland will be vindicated for the sins – crimes that was done to her in the days of old.

Germany has a debt to pay with God for which I will never forgive because they did burn the Jamaican Flag – the Flag of Life, hence I will infinitely and indefinitely never ever forgive them. I will not change this because I do hope Good God took notice of this and I truly know he did hence he asked me to write another book.

I cannot deviate from what I see via my dreams and or before me. I have to tell you hence you have these books.

As for the well known prince that keeps following me and telling me in my dreams that we are cousins. You said you trust me more than your family members including grandmother and mother. This according to my last dream but I say unto you in the living, I will not stand down from my stance cousin or not, family or not.

Know this. Billions of people are slated to die because of the lies of your ancestors. They are a part of the Abrahamic Code – Free Masons hence the illuminated ones. Things did not have to be this way. It did not have to come to this.

No one was slated to die but because of lies, the lies of your ancestors who followed the Nodite way of life hence your family's presence in Nod, the damage has been done.

What right did your family have to send billions to hell with their lies – book of lies – sin?

What right did your family have to sacrifice billions with their lies and deceit?

Good God never commissioned anyone to write the book of sin or translate the book of sin to take humanity to hell. We all know that hell is a prison and it is hot. Hell is the final death for many and what your family did was not right. Humanity cannot comprehend the heat of hell because they think the fire – heat of the sun is the fire of hell when it is not.

No human being can measure atomic fire (that's what I call the fire of hell). It is that hot because no one thinks that the spirit can burn. Energy does burn and it can be killed, but no human being can kill this energy because they have no power to do so. It is not for man to kill the spirit in that way. This job belongs to Sin hence the wages of sin is death. Sin is the death of flesh in the living and the death of spirit in the grave.

Condemning someone to hell is so not nice and like I said, billions have their DDC and there is nothing they can do to change this. When you can change your DC to a GLC you cannot change your DDC. Your DDC is your final death and like I said, it is not fair nor was it fair for your family to do this, commission the book of sin (the holy bible) to be written.

In all your trust and you reminding me that we are cousins, it means nothing to me because Good God and humanity did not deserve this.

Good God did nothing to your family or humanity. He God – Good God gave us good life and we are the ones to give it away – destroy it.

Someone comes and say, I will give you this because this is better but it's not better. We do not weigh the pros and cons nor do we think of the consequences. SIN HAS A CONSEQUENCE AND THAT CONSEQUENCE IS DEATH.

THE WAGES OF SIN IS DEATH AND WHEN WE DO SIN WE BECOME SINK AS WELL AS DIE.

I have to think about Good God and humanity. I have to think about the lie that was told hence God – Good God must save his own.

We all know that in all the devil gives he cannot maintain or sustain it because he's a giver backer taker. Each year you have to kill – make sacrifices unto the dead – death for you to maintain your status with sin – death. This is the reality of many of you but in the end you are going to die a harsh death because the death of flesh is nothing compared to the death of spirit. The death of spirit is your final extinction and your spirit have to burn in hell before it eventually dies.

There is no water in hell and some of you are saying this is fine it's just the spirit who cares. But I am telling you, truly care because you were told, "AS IT IS ON EARTH SO IT IS IN HEAVEN."

Heaven is not where Good God resides. Heaven is hell for those who truly know, except you are not dealing with the flesh you are dealing with the spirit.

The only difference with us and hell or heaven if you prefer is that there is no water in hell. The spirit requires water hence I've told you if you ask God – Good God to shower you with his blessings; he showers you with water because water is his blessings. Hence water is so abundant on earth as well as the beginning of life.

All the millions and billions he Satan has given he must take it back. You must lose it all because what he gave was not his to give in the first place.

Earth does not belong to death nor does it belong to Satan and the demons of hell. Earth belongs to Good God because earth is a part of Life – Good Life hence Earth is a part of Good God.

The harvest comes now and woe be unto many nations because all that the devil gave unto you, it must be taken away infinitely and indefinitely.

It is not God's or Good God's children that must fear this harvest.

It is not God's or Good God's children that will go hungry and penniless it is the devil's children. They must die.

Death must take them because in all they do, they do to kill and deceive – spread lies and hate throughout humanity.

Like I said, you all can hate me but I care not who hates me. At the end of the day I did that which was required of me by Good God. As long as I did my job truthfully and honestly I am good to go. I cannot care about the evil and wicked man and or person because it is them that go against Good God and his people.

It is them that seek to destroy all that Good God has and have given us.

It is them that tell you you must die to see God – Good God when they fully know that you cannot die to see Good God, you can only die to see death. You can only die to die a painful death in hell hence billions are slated to die on earth as well as in the spirit – the spiritual realm.

Life – good life goes up to see Good God it cannot go down to see death and we should all know this.

I've told you my homeland (Jamaica) has been deemed unclean by Good God and I cannot go back into the land.

I've shown you in A Little Little Talk – Book Two how I wanted to disobey Good God. I've shown you my struggles hence I am holding my peace because the day I go home is the day I would lose it all. It's not easy but you have to do that which God – Good God commands you to do. He's shown me my sin if I disobey him and I've shown you what our sins look like when we sin against God – disobey him. So it's up to each and every one of you to live clean and true.

We cannot say we are of God – Good God and live dirty. If we are living dirty we are not of God – Good God but of the devil – death.

Once again France and Canada you are duly warned because something is going to happen and Iran is going to come into play. You cannot play the Babylonian game that's all I have to say. I cannot tell you the full dream because I myself cannot comprehend it but be on guard. Neither of you cannot say you have not been warned because you have been warned.

As for you the BLACK NATIONS you now need to break away from ISLAM because WE ARE NOT UNDER THE BANNER OF BABYLON.

I know Ethiopia is because they were the first nation to JOIN THE BABYLONIAN UNION. They were the original Israelites that sold out Good God.

And yes Judah did the same thing because Judah followed them hence Judah – Yudah is unclean in the eyes and sight of Good God.

I feel sorry for none because we all know the way of the Babylonians. Hence we all fall down and die. Yes it's a song but we literally fall down and die in the end.

Time has no end but evil hath time hence the time to die. Good life cannot die nor can it concede to death because good life is separate from death. Hence good life has nothing to do with death.

The children of God – Good God know death hence we see death and tell you about death.

Many things we cannot explain because the time to explain it is not right.

Sometimes we see death clearly and sometimes we don't because death mask death and I've shown you and told you this in a lot of my books.

Sometimes we see the death of a female but in the living it is a male that dies hence you cannot easily pinpoint death.

I know there are many things that I have not told you in depth but I cannot because of timing meaning the time is not right.

Yes 1313 draws to a close and we are on the way to 2032 and I can infinitely and indefinitely confirm the end of man as being before 2032.

I've told you 2132 we lost and it has been confirmed that the end of man is before 2032 hence every wicked and evil system including animals and humans must go down in flames and die.

Evil must be no more and if you are not living clean and good, you will not make it past the harvest because the harvest is for the devil's people.

God's children – the children of Good God will not face this harvest, but if they fail to listen then they too must die. And as it is, because of the stubborn nature of BLACK PEOPLE hell is full of them and recruiting more black souls.

I do not want to get into the Lodge Man society because these societies are not of God – Good God but the devils own.

You have top feeders who are the billionaires of this world and then you have the bottom feeders who you call the illuminated ones – illuminati's or the children of the light. The illuminati's are the bottom feeders that mock the eye in the triangle. I will not get into the upright triangle because this symbol is a sacred symbol that these people know nothing about hence they mock God – Good God and his cleanliness as well as his righteousness. The devil and his people cannot be upright no matter what they do. They can only be downright hence they represent the downward triangle. They go down to hell hence they bathe in blood, drink blood and represent the dead. They literally kill hence the many sacrifices that they do and the money offerings that they have to give to keep their names out of the news. They have to buy protection from the devil's people hence you find many of them are going bankrupt. Hence I've told you the devil is a giver backer taker because all that he gives you, he wants it back.

He wants payment for his services and it matters not how you do it, he must have his money - paid.

He doesn't care if you take drugs – buy his drugs.

He doesn't care if you walk naked or perform all that is vulgar and unacceptable in the eyes and sight of Good God.

He does not care who you kill, sacrifice to keep him satisfied as long as you do it.

If he says your ass is mine you better know that your ass is truly his. You are his butt plug because you signed on the bottom line. You entered into a contract with sin and at the end of the day **_YOUR SOUL IS HIS_** and there's not a damned thing you can do about it. He has your name and number including your signature on his contract hence he owns you. All of you including your children.

The Star of David is the death star and I've told you this. This star represents the marriage of Good and Evil hence this star is not good, it can only be evil.

It's just like the church mocking the cross of death because true demons use the cross – inverted cross. A true Satanist or demon wears the inverted cross and triangle because their life is down and their home is down. So when I see these people pointing up I say wow, you are truly pointing down because your life is down – in hell with the demons of hell.

I flip everything around HENCE TIME WILL TELL. YOU THINK YOU'RE IN HEAVEN BUT YOU'RE TRULY LIVING IN HELL. NONE OF YOU WILL ESCAPE HELL.

If you believe in the trinity and praise and worship the trinity – THE THREE DADS – TRINIDAD you are hell bound. Hence hell is your home and will forever be your home. You believe and worship death hence there is no escaping death for many of you.

Yes there is a lot more but because time is winding down, I have to leave certain things alone because wow.

Dear God the book of death. Many of you think your name is in the book of life but your name is not in the book of life, it is in the book of death.

As for you Jamaica have mercy Lord because death will walk and claim its own shortly. I cannot give you a specific date and time but you – the people and land of Jamaica is done. The devil is almost out of jail and woe be unto the lots of you. *YOU'VE ALL UNDONE WHAT BOB MARLEY HAS DONE WHEN IT COMES TO THE MUSIC HENCE A LOT OF YOU RALLY AROUND THE MUSIC OF DEATH – DANCEHALL.*

Aidonia you are no different because I see the tattoo on your back.

The door has been opened to the lots of you but by the grace of God – Good God, I am closing the door to the lots of you.

Yes many of you will want to hurt me but you cannot kill me because I do not walk in the valley of the dead like many of you.

I do not pay the dead like many of you. I see the dead, hence I can talk about the dead including the living and walking dead – zombies that have human flesh.

Aidonia keep following the truck of death – dancehall because many of you will fall and must fall hence death awaits many of you. You have a tattoo that I've never seen before. I can't find the image in Google to show you what your tattoo looks like. I know I've seen something similar to it in a movie. I'm not sure if it's a Spiderman or Batman or X Men movie. It's the character with the muzzle mask. Your mark or tattoo that the beast gave you is similar to this muzzle mask.

Many of you have tattoos and say it's harmless but I've told you anything given to the devil – Satan he keeps. He play for keeps and many of you have lost your soul because billions upon billions of you have the mark of the beast and it's no joke.

Your body is sacred and you are not to put tattoos or henna on your skin. This is an abominable sin hence when death comes death must and will take you.

I've told you about Cain in another book hence God did not mark Cain. Cain had his father's birthmark and I've told you this. I've also told you Satan has no male child. THE CHILDREN OF DEATH WERE TRIPLETS – 3 BEAUTIFUL MIXED CHILDREN THAT WALKED IN UNISON. I've told you what the mark in their foreheads look like and I've also told you the timeframe or timeline of death.

Like I said, a new war is brewing and the United States of America will not escape this judgement because their empire is going to come a tumbling down. America did align itself with the devil hence they fight the devil's wars.

Russia has its mandate meaning it's time because they were warned in Blackman Redemption – The Death of Russia. If they do not heed the warning of God – Good God, they too will end up like America. They will lose it all because like I said, God – Good God did send Marcus Mosiah Garvey to teach Americans about enterprise and because he was a black man, they did all to make him fail including slander him. So because America did not listen America must fall.

Their stink hole of a sinkhole called their NATIONAL DEBT is a testament of this – them not listening to the messenger of God – Good God.

Sometimes it is good to listen. Go back to your book of sin (holy bible) and read about Noah. Noah tried to warn the people and they did not listen. They cussed Noah to scorn and did all manner of things to him. They said it was not going to rain but the rain came didn't it? Now tell me how many was saved?

We are no different today because we are not listening.

But I go to church and give 1/10th of my earnings to the church you are saying.

Good for you because you are giving death his pay to not kill you. Death is going to kill you because death can only be loyal to death.

No one can pay for life or pay God – Good God for life. He Good God gave you life good and true. You are the one to give it to death.

That 1/10th you are giving to death (the churches) give it to a homeless shelter.

If you don't want to give it to a homeless shelter and you have family in need, buy some groceries for that family or use the money to pay down a debt for them.

If that is not your cup of tea then buy some groceries and give it to a food bank. If that is not your cup of tea and if you travel buy some medical supplies, pens, pencils, erasers, books, crayons, even pampers and give to a local hospital or school. Do not be selfish but do something.

Yes you can even send a money order or cheque to your local government and tell them that

$5.00 or $10.00 is to pay down their state or provincial debt. I've told you this already.

If you do not have $5.00 or $10.00 to give then pray to Good God in a clean and true manner. Clean prayers are accepted by God – Good God and dirty ones are rebuked – repelled.

Well I don't believe in God and he does not exist some of you are saying.

God – Good God does exist. He is not made up nor is he man made to control you. He is there for each one of us but he cannot continue to be. He's giving you time to truly come on board. Meaning save yourself if you want to be saved.

Like I've said and will forever ever tell you. Good God does not shut anyone out of his abode, we are the ones to shut ourselves out with our lies – sins.

No he's not you're saying. You've doubt his existence you're saying. TRUE but he does exist.

Listen God – Good God cannot reside with us and beat the crap out of the devil for us. Trust me if he could come into earth and do all for us he would. This I've learned the hard and harsh way.

I've told you God – Good God cannot come into this planet because it is riddled with sin meaning earth has and have become dirty due to the sins of man – humanity. So because of this God – Good God cannot come in to earth nor can he reside with us. All he Good God can do is put things in time and wait for us as humans to catch up to that point in time.

And yes, the more we sin is the longer it is for us to catch up to that point in time.

This is why we say God is slow but he's sure and I've told you this in another book.

Evil controls earth.
Evil conditions and controls hence we are controlled beings.

We are the ones to want what the devil has.
We are the ones to say yes to the devil.

We are the ones that live for wants instead of living for needs. Wants are not needs hence we do all that is evil to get what we want and not what we need.

We see the devil's children with the big houses and say I want that, but do we truly need it?

How about a Condo? Just having that 3 or 4 bedroom condo with a patio where you can plant your flowers and tomatoes?

Yes you pay for maintenance fee to keep the place clean but think about it. You don't have to mow the lawn or clean the snow.

In life do you and do you good and clean. If you are living a clean life no matter your sexual orientation and you are giving from the goodness of your heart, then you have nothing to worry about.

Well what about my soul because the bible says this and that you are saying.

Do you because God – Good God is not a religion and I've told you this. I've also told you, no one can tell you what relationship to have with God – Good God.

But I want to get married and the church won't marry me.

Why would you want a dirty man to marry you?

The law and laws of God – Good God is not the law and laws of man. It is of God – Good God and it is Good God that you need to worry about. Well not worry about because no one can worry about Good God this I know. Once you know him you can worry about his well being.

Listen and listen clearly because I've told you this. If you want to have a place with Good God then live clean good and true.

If you are divorced by man go to God – Good God and ask for a divorce from him before you marry another person or get involved with someone else. I did not know this before but I know this now, hence I've gotten my divorce from all the men I've ever lain with from Good God. I am now clean hence I can get involved with another human being.

You cannot take another person as a wife or mate if you are not divorced from God – Good God.

Listen to me further now. If you have not asked Good God for a divorce and a member of the clergy remarries you, then that person that remarries you is infinitely and indefinitely responsible for your sin – adultery. That clergy person who remarries you has and have sinned _and he too will be charged worse than you for sin – guilt. He or She caused you to sin against God – Good God. That clergy or Justice of the Peace member have and has sinned against God – Good God hence he or she is held guilty of sin in lieu of you. It does not mean your slate is clean or you will not be held accountable for sin as well. But the blunt or burden of sin falls upon the person that remarries you. They represent God – Good God hence certain things they are to truly know. Hence they did not do their job and they are not of God – Good God but of the devil. They are doing the work of the devil so worry not if they don't want to marry you._

A TRUE MARRIAGE IS A COMMITMENT of truth between you and God not you and man. A marriage of commitment cannot be broken by you or God – Good God because it is a commitment and it is from everlasting to everlasting.

So if you say you are committed to your partner you better not cheat on him or her.

You better not be stingy.

You had better not be a gold digger.

You had better work together to build each other in a clean, true and good way.

All the lies you are accustomed to, you cannot do hence a committed relationship or marriage is not for everyone.

What if I fall out of love with him or her?

Then you were never true to him or her because you cannot fall out of love if you love true. True love is an everlasting love. It is a bond with God – Good God hence true love is rare. One cannot love true and the other love.

True love has nothing to do with greed or financial gain.

If the both of you live in a cardboard box, then each one put a penny each towards savings to come out of that cardboard box.

It matters not if he has pants that are torn as long as he has ambition and is working to sew that torn pants. You both do it together and continue growing till you grow up to God – Good God. It does take time hence I tell you true love is rare.

But you got to work at it.

Hell no. Who told you that?

You work at love not true love. True love is free and it is natural. There is no outdoing each other you grow. This growth is good.

Let me stop here. Wow because this book is the end of man. Anyone that says they have to work at true love is a damned liar this I know. Hence I tell you if you need a good woman or man in your life bug God – Good God for that person. He will find that individual for you. It will take him time because he has to weed through the ruffians of earth to find that good and true person for you. I've told you this hence I am still waiting.

Soon though and trust me I will tell you about it hence I tell you to know your colours and your tree of life.

Everyone has a tree of life so know what your tree of life is. God – Good God will show you that person using your tree of life. And yes this is why the tree of life is in Genesis the book of sin. Remember the devil seek to take all from God – Good God so know the truth not just believe it.

This book in titled the end of man.

1313 which I say is 2013 is coming to a close and woe be unto humanity.

I know I have not told you how man will die because I've covered the death of man or the end of man in my other books.

This new war that is coming will signal the end of man – humanity. The end of man is for wicked and evil systems; wicked and evil lands including people.

Now to get truly off course and racist because you all know I am capable of racism.

As for you the different races that hate BLACK PEOPLE.

As for you the different races of the different clergy that say BLACKS ARE INFERIOR.

All of you can kiss my natural brown ass and go F yourselves.

Yes I went there.

Duly go back to your book of sin (Revelations) and SEE THE RACE AND OR COLOUR JESUS IS.

According to your book of sin Jesus was not a Pale Jew but a Black Jew with hair like Wool – Nappy Ass hair hence MARY HIS MOTHER WAS BLACK.

NOW PUT IT TOGETHER.

<u>**SINCE THE SON OF GOD – GOOD GOD ACCORDING TO YOUR BOOK OF SIN IS BLACK, THEN GOD – GOOD GOD IS BLACK.**</u>

So the lots of you are worshipping and bowing down to a BLACK GOD.

Booyaca, Booyaca.

So eat them sour grapes, apple, and bitter lemon and lime bitch.

Sorry Good God but I had to go there. I know the truth and the end of everything but today I could not help it. I had to rub it in because in truth YOU'VE NEVER CHOSEN A WHITE PERSON TO DELIVER YOUR MESSAGE at least not that I am aware of. I do not know if it's because of the curse that was put on them. You alone know and one day you will show me the truth from the beginning of their history.

I know not all whites belong to the white race but some belong to the black race hence they fall under the banner of black – good life but I so could not help the above.

I know whites reside on the second level of the triangle. Not many but they are still with you so please forgive me, but I so wanted to stick it to the racist clergy bastards that are out there.

Saying Blacks are inferior. So Good God if BLACKS ARE INFERIOR then that would make you INFERIOR ALSO. They are saying you are inferior because you fall under the banner of black.

Come on now Good God look into it. You are black because the light cannot comprehend the darkness – blackness of the universe including earth and you. So because you are under the banner of black and you fall in the category of black, then are they not saying you are inferior too? Truly look into it.

Now I ask you this Good God. If your people – black people are inferior and like I said, you are black, who is going to save these racist bastards from hell?

No for real Good God. We the black race are inferior according to them. Then who is going to save these racist bastards because I am telling you this right now, I will not do it.

Yes I delivered the message you gave me to give to Russia and South Africa. My job is done insofar as that goes, but I still have a lot more work to do I know this, but I do need a break, yes a vacation.

Come on Good God who do some of these people think they are? Hence I dedicate TIME WILL TELL BY ROBERT NESTA MARLEY TO THE LOTS OF THEM.

Your children will never weep because you did remember South Africa and I hope Black South Africans know this. Because as Bob Marley said, "Jah would never give the power to a bald head." Yes many think they are in heaven but they are truly living in hell. Hell bound because of the sins they do on a daily basis.

Tell me something Good God. Who amongst man – humanity can say they know you other than me? Yes I am being a brat now because I know many can say they know you hence you have your good seeds that you must look after. Come on now.

Blacks inferior and we are the ones to hold the Ark of the Covenant.

We were the ones to take life out of Egypt – the now Egypt and bring it as far as China where it resides until this day. This covenant the Chinese call the Ying Yang. Come on now.

Humanity knows not life hence all evil life must come to an end. Evil had 24 000 years to deceive and destroy and evil did his job. Evil used sin to bring humanity to their deaths. Humanity did follow blindly now billions are on the payroll of death, hence shortly they will die. They must die with sin and death because you Good God did find the one that you needed to tell the truth and carry on your goodness and truth. She will rise and when she does Satan will quake because in truth, he has no power. She does hence the XX when it comes to evil – evil genes.

True evil cannot change hence the good they do is looked upon as evil because there is no good in evil, just pure and utter evil – deceit.

Yes many will learn the hard way hence many of your children will be caught up in the killing field that is to come.

Time does tell hence in all we do, it's done in time at a point in time.

Now back to the racist bastards of this world. I will not save them because they hate you and me. ***They hate my people hence I will not plea for them because their hatred is genuine – pure.*** I will however take responsibility for the seeds – good and true people that you have given me. Hence I call them my family. They are our family of goodness and truth. I have to help them and ensure they are right and safe with you in all that they do.

Yes I have to take responsibility for you too Good God because despite me cussing you and getting down hard on you, you are my true love and you are a part of my true family. Hence you are a part of my good and true family tree.

I know there is a better way in life and you are that better way hence you protect me so much. You do not allow me to walk or go in the pathway of the unclean and I truly thank you for this.

As 1313 comes to a close I thank you for my lessons learned.

I thank you for my ups and downs.

I thank you for holding on to me and not allowing me to fall at the hands of evil.

Thank you for letting me overcome my obstacles in 1313 and it is my hope that you will make 2014 better, more rewarding and prosperous in all that is good and true for me.

I know the true love I have for Jamaica and like I've said, I will not cry or plead for the people. But I will however, cry and plead to you for the land. I truly love our little Island of Judah – You. Death can take his people but we must clean up Jamaica for me and you.

Like South Africa, I want to do a lot more for Jamaica. So if it be thy will spare the land of Jamaica but let death take his wicked and evil people. Leave the good people of the land but every wicked human being, including animal and child as well as evil spirit, must be condemned to hell. Hence they must go do to hell immediately and burn.

Listen Good God; I need to walk in goodness and in truth with you forever ever. No there is no until death do us part. That's death. Good can never part nor can good die, so give death his pay. You cannot continue to save death's children. You have to save the children of good and truth hence come 2014 let the empires of evil and death be no more.

Let them crumble and fall.

It's time for goodness now come on now. 24 000 years Good God aid if we haven't learnt by now, we will never learn.

There is life and there is death. We are to choose life and live.

Michelle Jean

Life isn't all about giving, it's about receiving also. Hence the spiritual world is complex for those who don't know it.

As humans we talk about death hence we only know the death of flesh and not the death of spirit.

Life is not a joke hence many live in lies for lies.

I've asked this question before. If the lie did not work for Eve (Evening) how is it going to work for you?

Eve was lied to. She didn't become a god.

She died.

She died spiritually because she was not able to communicate with God.

She also got kicked out of the realm of God because she did sin. She disobeyed God hence losing her soul and place with God.

Satan was already unclean hence she became unclean also.

She became death because she's the one to sit at the gate (s) of hell and receive her wicked and evil children. Yes disobedient children who follow after sin and all manner of evil.

She died a spiritual death then a physical death to die another spiritual death once the time of sin and evil on earth is over. This is the final death and trust me this death is harsh and painful. This is the reality of virtually every human being that resides on earth right now.

Earth must change her cycle for the better and in doing so she must take away her grace and mercy – food and water from the wicked at heart. This time around good must separate from all evil. If this does not happen, then alot of good people will be caught up in this war. Many will die because they did not listen – heed the warnings and cries of Good God.

Like I've said, I've seen the war and I've seen the ripe tomatoes that became spoilt on the ground. They did not escape the war. They were slaughter – killed.

It's an old war hence it's a new war that is going to start.

Like I said Americans will not escape this judgement because all they do is lie and kill, aide Babylon in their wars and fight – death. They truly kill without knowing that a good and clean Muslim can and will be saved because they call on Allah which means the Breath of life five times per day.

They bow down to the Breath of Life and they America aide in the deceitful ones – Kafares – Jinns and Janns of Islam that say they are Muslim but are the devil's own kill Life – Kill the Breath of Life directly and indirectly.

Please note the saving grace is given to those who have converted to Islam and no the other way around. This is how I saw it and this is how I am relating it back to you.

Islam is a spiritual prison hence you were told in my other book (s) hell is full of Black People and recruiting more.

Satan, Death, Melchesidec isn't concerned about his people because they are locked in hell already. ***He's concerned about the Black Race hence he tries to destroy BLACKS BY ANY MEANS NECESSARY.*** Blacks are the only race that is hated globally by every nation on earth including their own race – blacks.

Eliminating blacks will not save anyone. It just makes your nation become extinct quickly.

Meaning you are locking yourself infinitely and indefinitely out of Good God's kingdom – domain.

Truly take a look at the Ying and Yang and see life for yourself, hence the Chinese reside at the base of God's – Good God's mountain.

Absolutely no one can say they are going to see God or Allah or Good God and hate. God – Good God – Allah – Allelujah – Jah gave us the breath of life and like I've said time and time again, we are the ones to give it away to sin.

Absolutely no sin can get you into Good God's Kingdom hence billions die to see death. I've told you this. I've also told you no one can die to see life, you have to live it (life) good, clean and true.

No religion of any kind can get you into Good God's kingdom or home because He and She Good God – Allah – Allelujah – Jah – Alleluya did not give us religions of men to deceive self and spirit.

No one on the face of this planet can tell you what religion Good God is because he and she is not a religion.

No one can rely on religion because religion lie and deceive and I've told you this.

If religion could save man – humanity including your spirit MY HOMELAND WOULD NOT HAVE BEEN DEEMED UNCLEAN BY GOD – GOOD GOD.

Jamaica has many churches for which people attend but yet the island was deemed unclean. Hence you now know and know that religion cannot save anyone.

This did not have to be this way but unfortunately this is the way it is. Like I said, God – Good God is teaching me, hence I have to teach you no matter how hurtful things are to me and you.

Remember I did not deem Jamaica unclean, God – Good God deemed it so and told me so. Hence you need to know what is unclean and clean in the eyes and sight of God – Good God.

You need to know what makes you unclean in his eyes. By you saying you go to church and give 10% of your earnings does not make you clean. It means you are aiding sin as well as paying sin to kill you.

I've told you, you have to live for God – Good God but I've since learnt you cannot live for God or Good God, you have to live clean and good – true and honest for you.

As long as you are living clean good and true you are good to go because you are not only honouring you, you are honouring God – Good God. No one can tell you how to live your good and clean as well as true life for Good God. No that's not true, I should say no dirty person including beast, spirits and child can tell you how to live for Good God.

Remember evil does not want you to succeed. Evil wants you to fail hence I am going to tell you to go back to Ambush in the Night and Babylon System by Bob Marley. You need to know that the devil has his system as well and a part of that system is the government – political systems of the world including major organizations that rape the earth of her wealth.

They kill her and take what does not belong to them. They kill her trees and pollute her waterways hence Mother Earth is no different from us humans.

Good life was given we are the ones to make it unclean.

We are the ones that must now clean up ourselves and become right in the eyes and sight of God – Good God.

He Good God has nothing to do with death he has all to do with life.

THE END OF MAN DRAWS NEAR AND IT'S UP TO YOU TO CHANGE YOU AND LIVE CLEAN BECAUSE THIS HARVEST IS GOING TO BE BRUTAL FOR MANY.

THE END OF MAN – HUMANITY – EVIL'S SYSTEM OF THINGS IS BEFORE 2032 HENCE YOU NOW HAVE YOUR MANDATE TO ELIMINATE SOME OF SINS THAT IS ON YOUR SLATE.

I did tell you I saw Black and White Death side by side and they had the scroll of death.

One had it in his hands so death is preparing to read the names that are on death's death list.

So truly good luck to billions of you because I can tell you the names of some of you literally.

Many of you in the entertainment industry can kiss your life in the spiritual realm goodbye literally because many of you signed on the dotted line of death hence you have your Death's Death Certificate.

This is permanent and nothing good that you do will be looked upon as good. It is looked upon as evil and is evil because you are mocking good literally. And many of you do mock good when you desecrate and pose up the upright triangle as well as upright eye in the triangle. Trust me Good God is waiting for many of you hence some of you were called out in some of these books because Good God is not having it.

You cannot desecrate God – Good God and mock him in all that you do. This is not right hence the world is going to quake because all who you think is not a part of the devil's domain is. Like I said, the devil's power is temporary hence God – Good God does not deal in death he deals in life literally.

Everything that you've read about in the book of sin has been fulfilled because sin did his job.

IT WAS NOT EVE (EVENING) ALONE DEATH – SIN OR SATAN LIED TO. HE LIED TO HUMANITY BUT ITS HUMANITY THAT FAILED TO SEE THIS.

He told you God gave Cain a mark but it's not Cain alone that has the mark of sin – death. Many in life – earth has this mark hence billions of you are tattooed freaks. Many of you have and has accepted the mark of the beast – his tattoos. Yes you're all the agents and children of death so if you don't know now you know.

You can correct this for those that want to but for some the tattoo goes further.

Spiritual tattoo's you cannot change.

Meaning those that have gotten the spiritual mark of the beast, meaning the mark of the beast in the spiritual realm, you cannot change this mark in the living because you are a part of the devil's domain literally in the spiritual and physical.

You are a part of the dead hence death has you and your children including friends and family locked in hell. There is no escaping this judgement for any of you. You literally have your DDC ALREADY AND NOT EVEN GOOD GOD CAN CHANGE THIS. He infinitely and indefinitely forever ever literally cannot change this. This I more than know.

Sin did his job now the harvest comes and truly woe be unto man – humanity literally.

Go back to Redemption Song by Bob Marley. He talked about fulfilling the book and I've asked what book do we have to fulfill in another book?

We did not have to fulfill the book of sin but we did anyway.

This harvest did not have to come but because we live to sin and tell lies, our death

must come not just physically but spiritually.

I've told you we can hear the dead cry but because of the noise around us we cannot.

Trust me if we could and some of us can, we would not do some of the shit we do on a daily basis. The dead do walk and some even recruit other death (evil) dead to kill you. This I know for an infinite and indefinite fact and no one, not even God – Good God can say this is a lie because I know the truth, seen the truth and have told you the truth. And for some of you that say this is a lie, duppy or the dead do come into your home. They are in some of our homes. The Good one lets you know they are in your home because they slam the cupboard door; drop pot covers on the floor, bang on the wall or door including the floor to make you know that they are there. Some of us our spirits rise meaning get goose bumps as you call them when spirit – the dead is around. Some of you even see them face to face literally and I've told you this.

Like I've said, true love cannot lie nor can it deceive, hence I do not deal in love I deal in true love.

True love is the highest form of life and truth anyone can have because this truth – true love is rare as well as truly godly – of Good God.

Evil cannot handle true love because evil deals in love. When you truly love you do not want to be amongst love or lovers of love. You want and need to be amongst true love – true lovers meaning Good God.

You want to be with him daily talking to him, doing good things for him. You like planting trees, bathing or swimming in the river that he has and have given, you want and need to live good and true hence you try to do things good and true all the time.

At times you just want to sit there looking at nature saying God – Good God is this truly you?

You want to live free and give to others freely.

You don't like fighting or killing hence you want to separate yourself from wicked and evil people – the sinners of this world.

When you love true you are not governed by greed or religion, you are governed by truth which is the goodness of God – Good God.

Also for those that are trying to walk freely with God – Good God, make sure you have at least one lime tree in your backyard or front yard. A lime tree – organic lime tree is a must.

I cannot explain it but you must have it on your property. And no lime isn't sour it's aromatic. Just boil a couple of leaves and you will see.

You can boil the leaves 2 or 3 and drink the water – so good for the body. But if you don't want to drink the water after boiling that's fine. Just inhale the aroma trust me it's that fragrant.

Onwards I go but before I proceed, pull up Misty Morning by Duane Stephenson and truly listen to this song. This song goes out to all my enemies whether living or dead, my spiritual enemies, my enemies in the flesh, the enemies of God – Good God because it's you alone that want to live. All others must die and you have it all but you cannot have it all because God – Good God did not give evil this earth to conquer.

Nor did he give it to you to control and dominate.

I also dedicate this song to Good God also because this morning December 20, 2013 I dreamt yet again that my financial prosperity was been taken from me and I am getting fed up of this crap. All of 2013 my financial prosperity was taken from me and now at the end it's being taken from me again.

So Good God I ask you yet again. WHY DO YOU NOT WANT ME TO BE SUCCESSFUL FINANCIALLY IN LIFE?

WHY RIGHT DO YOU HAVE TO TAKE MY WEALTH FROM ME?

Yes I am tired of begging at your table for the crumbs of life hence I tell you, if you do not mean me any good to leave me the Fuck alone because I am getting tired of this.

I will not beg you anymore for anything because I refuse to be your prostitute begging you for anything anymore. I am not a fucking cocaine or crack addict that I have to beg you like a wanting dog for everything.

Like I said, you are a good protector but when it comes to my prosperity you have failed me time and time again and I am fed up of it. If you do not want or need good for me and if you do not mean me and my family any good leave us the fuck alone. One cannot be trying to do good and you are breaking them down all the time. It means you are not clean nor do you have any goodness in you for that person.

I am tired of it with you hence Misty Morning is literally and truly dedicated to you because IT'S YOU ALONE THAT WANT TO LIVE. If you wanted me to succeed in life in a good and true way you would not be literally hindering me. SO I NOW ASK YOU GOOD GOD, WHY ARE YOU TAKING MY PROSPERITY FROM ME?

You cannot ask someone to write you a book twice but yet give them the tools to fail in the long run. This isn't truth nor is it true love it's hatred on your part. Like I said, I will not lie for you and in doing so I have to live clean and make my life happy. I've told you, you truly do not make me happy. And in all honesty I truly do not know why you want and need me to fail. If failing is what you want of me then by all means I will do it out of spite and go to Jamaica the land that you deemed unclean so you of yourself can fail. Like I've said, your failure rate is high when it comes to your messengers and this is because of you. You do not give them the right tools to succeed hence they are hindered at every turn and I refuse to be like any of them. I refuse to be your bitch because what you do to your messengers is not right. You are wrong in your dealings and treatment of them. It's as if you want us to lie for you and like I said, I refuse to do that. Hence I've told you I refuse to convert anyone to you because no one can be converted to good and true life you have to live it. You have to live your life good and clean so stop shutting me up. Stop locking away and stop locking up my prosperity because it's not yours it's mine. You cannot take away my prosperity and lock it up like it matters not to me. It matters to me because I am struggling financially, emotionally, health wise and spiritually.

I am not a demon seed hence I have hope. You cannot take my wealth from me man come on now. I do not do it to you so don't do it to me. I'm not just trying for me I am trying for both of us. I need you to hold your head up in truth but you want me to hold my head down in shame and disgrace. Come on now how does that work? How does that work between me and you? So yes I dedicate Misty Morning to you yet again and ask you why? Why are you taking my good life, my physical and spiritual wealth and prosperity away from me?

Why should I live and die alone and you be happy like I do not exist or mean anything to you?

Stop feeding me and giving me lies – false hope when it comes to my life because I do not do it to you. I am more than truthful to you but from your actions with me, I truly have to wonder if you deserve me.

Yes I went there because in all that I've been doing to build you and me including my family – our family, you take it all from me. Every route and road that I take you shut all the doors in my face.

All the roads I've taken have sink holes in them.

So far you haven't opened any doors for me. I'm shut down so tell me who's failing whom, you or me?

You cannot lock away my future because you are hindering me from doing the good that I need and want to do.

IN TRUTH GOOD GOD FROM THE WAY I SEE IT YOU ARE THE ONE TO LOCK YOUR CHILDREN AWAY FROM GOODNESS BECAUSE YOU DO NOT WANT TO SEE ANY OF US PROSPER.

Prosperity for you people was never in the book of life so now I ask you this. How the hell can you say you are life – good life and truth when truth was never in you from the beginning?

No this is not doubt this is my truth and true feelings of you.

You are Allelujah – the Breath of Life but yet you imprison the Breath of Life in the flesh and in the spirit. Yes I can blame the devil but you know what Good God you are to blame as well. The devil isn't the only guilty one in all of this, you are guilty also.

Yes I've been making excuses for you and it stops here. I will not make excuses anymore for you because I know time and the distance and or length in time. I know the communication method used in the living and in the spiritual realms.

I know about cleanliness and in all that I've done, is excuse you and I refuse to do it anymore because you can do better, you just don't want to. You refuse to.

You are like those fathers that ignore their children and expect us to find the answers and solutions to our problems by ourselves.

Like I said, I refuse to excuse you from anything anymore because you can do better. Hence you can only love us so and not love us true or truly love us.

Yes you are good in many ways but I had to vent because of what I saw. Plus I keep dreaming that I am at the store searching for a particular package of Paper Mate Pens but cannot find that package. I found Paper Mate Pens but some are 2 to a package, 4 to a package but mainly 4 to package. I wanted the 10 to a package. Suffice it to say I ended up never getting any of the pens. So something is not right someplace because I can't get what I want. This is the second day in a row that I am having this dream and I am getting fed up of it because I so do not know what this dream means.

You as God and Good God know that I like Paper Mate Pens and they must come 10 to a package. I will not change or stray from this because I do not like using BIC Pens anymore. I use to truly love BIC Pens but because of her and the use of BIC I feel uncomfortable using that line of pens. She just demonized the brand hence I go the Paper Mate route because I know trees – Paper and your true love and passion for writing. Everything with you must be written hence your words have been written throughout the ages by your chosen few.

Onwards go now.

God is good all the time hence I rep Good God whenever I can.

Yes you can say God – Good God does not exist and if you've read my other books I've doubt him and cussed him, beat him up, told him bad words and you'll know this because I've made God – Good God my everything not just in the physical but in the spiritual realm as well. I'm not afraid to lay my cards out on the line with him and I've done this. Virtually all the books in the Michelle Jean line of books show you this.

Listen I've told you, like you I am learning hence the difference in spiritual time and physical time. I know the difference hence I've said I am not going to make excuses for God – Good God anymore because he makes none for us.

Yesterday is significant in spiritual time because yesterday is 3 – 9 months in time. Physical time must catch up to yesterday. Yes the time frame of yesterday could be longer than 3 – 9 months but I know it to be 3 – 9 months.

Lost my train of thought there meaning off course again.

Like I said, you can say God or Good God does not exist and you have all right to say that because I've said it. But God – Good God does exist. Remember I told you my homeland Jamaica is unclean and I cannot go into the land. If I go back to Jamaica I would be committing sin – grave sin and I would be like Eve. Trust me death would have a field day with me in hell. The fire and pit that is outlined for Satan and Sin including Death himself would be mild compared to mine. My pit in hell would be infinitely and indefinitely hotter than theirs.

Trust me the party in hell would be an infinite party because all Death has to do is point to me or at me and say God we have her. You lost – failed because here she is.

We win. We won against you.

Trust me Death and the hosts of hell would literally laugh at God and say another one bites the dust.

Wow have mercy Lord because the singing and dancing not even the Tatty, One Drop, Wata Pumpie, daggering would or could compare to Death's dance because death's hand will be forever pointing at me saying you're mine now bitch.

All wey yu sey bout mi an noa bout mi yu cum yahso? You disappoint me. I thought you would make it because you of all people know better hence I was hoping you would have done better.

Truss mi it would be the first time nuff a unnu si duppy and demon laugh kek kem kem in di living literally.

Woe what a lala fi mi because hell would more than rejoice if mi get dey.

Yes Jamaica can be cleaned. Lysol (yellow bottle) was what I was shown to clean the island. Meaning Jamaica must become 99.9 percent clean. All the germs – sins of the people (the killing, sexual assaults of young girls and boys, the paedophilic activities must change; the corruption of police and government must change; the scamming and more must change – stop). And no not Pine Sol but Lysol. Once again Jamaica must become 99.9 percent clean before I can go back on the island. Meaning the willful killings for sport and otherwise must stop because at the end of the day, Jamaica is on the verge of sinking like Port Royal did in June of 1692. So Jamaica duly note: your land is on the chopping block. If ***THE ISLAND DOES NOT SINK IN FEBRUARY OF 2014, KNOW THAT MANY OF YOU WILL STARVE BECAUSE NO ONE CAN DO BUSINESS OR HELP YOUR ISLAND. THE ISLAND WAS DEEMED UNCLEAN BY GOD – GOOD GOD HIMSELF. TO DISOBEY GOD – GOOD GOD IS A GRAVE SIN AND TRUST ME I DON'T WANT TO BE ANYONE THAT DO THIS BECAUSE THEY WILL***

BE HELL BOUND. HELL WILL HAVE NO MERCY OR LIMIT AS TO HOW THEY INFLICT PUNISHMENT ON THE PERSON. HENCE EVERYONE IS DULY WARNED. SO TRULY GOOD LUCK.

The glorifying of Uncle and Daddy Demon and his cohorts must stop.

No more Gully Side or Gaza or Alliance – warring factions must be on the island. All these artists are doing is capturing your souls – spirit and giving it to the demons of hell, hence they are soul catchers of the worst and demonic kind.

The having unnecessary children must stop.

The killing of innocent children including babies must stop.

The raping of little children must stop.

The incest must stop.
The worshipping of Babylonian religions – deities and idols must stop because none of God's – Good God's children are Pagan.

The gay bashing must stop because Good God does not stop anyone from truly loving another human being – person. If Good God does not want you to be with someone he will use your tree of life to let you know. Hence I tell you all to know what your tree of life is.

Your tree of life is significant to life not death. When you go against your tree of life then you are going against life – God literally and you will die. Infinitely and indefinitely trust me on that hence the book of sin tells you about the tree of life. Eve went against her tree of life – teachings of God – Good God hence she died.

The fight over politics – this political and that political party must stop because Good God did not give any one politics to kill each other or the next man or person over. Go back to Ambush in the Night by Bob Marley and hear what he told you what must happen by these political party for you to have or get some food. Trust me these politicians think they are safe but it's only a fool that leave his people – the people of his homeland starving and in need that thinks he or she is safe in hell. ***Every politician is responsible for the people and children of***

the land. Down to the animals they are responsible for. And if they neglect any they will be neglected in hell. Meaning I truly don't want to be any in hell.

**If your land has two million people and you are not just to one million then your time in hell will be one million years times 24 000 years which equals 24 000 000 000 years. Plus on top of that add the penalty of each sin you committed against your people plus any interest or additional years death tacks on to your time in hell for good measure. So truly good luck to some of you politicians because your time in hell's fire will be brutal especially those who send men and women on the battle field to kill. Truly good luck because like I said, death of flesh is nothing compared to Spiritual**

death. Spiritual death is your final death and you have to spend time in hell before your spirit dies. The more the sin the more time you spend in hell.

So for those that have their DDC already truly good luck to you in hell because like I've said, you have no saving grace whatsoever.

To you that give your life over to death good luck because you have no saving grace whatsoever once your flesh or body touch the grave. So truly change your life for the better in the living before you go down in the grave.

I've told you there is a Black Death and a White Death and White Death is final death hence many say whites are superior but I say death is death.

Onwards I go

Jamaica the gang violence must stop because not everyone can like everybody. Not even Good God likes everyone. And no I am not lying. God – Good God does not like sin nor does he like death because he is good is true life even if I say otherwise sometimes.

He Good God does not like any form of violence or domestic abuse.

Sin loves violence because sin must control and dominate you.

Sin must beat you in order to control and dominate you.

Sin must enslave you.

Sin must pollute you with his lies so that you die – go to hell and die.

Sin must use you to do his will in order to keep Good God from entering or coming near earth.

Sin must keep you hungry, starving and wanting for food in order to control and dominate you.

Sin must kill you. This is the reality of every human being on the face of the planet who have sinned.

Many things Jamaica must do to come back to. They have a life line hence they must live by that life line forever ever hence they will lose it all.

Yes many is going to starve because like I said, the land is deemed unclean by Good God and the windows and doors of God – Good God are boarded up – closed. Hence it is up to every Jamaican to clean themselves up and open the windows and doors of and to Good God once again. Trust me it won't be easy because Judah – Jamaica did whore and sin like the Israelites of old.

You all know now that the island is unclean so if you are living clean and good for Good God and self you cannot go to Jamaica for any reason including death.

If you do, you will become unclean hence you will be like the rotten tomatoes of my dream. You will die. There are no ands ifs or buts about this.

IF YOU DISOBEY GOD – GOOD GOD YOU ARE GOING TO DIE. YOU MUST DIE BECAUSE YOU DID GO AGAINST GOD – GOOD GOD AND HIS WORDS.

If you are unclean and care not about your soul – spirit then this message is not for you. You can go because you do not know God – Good God nor do you respect or trust him.

In Good God deeming Jamaica unclean you cannot do business with them – meaning buy their goods – product. Nor can you have their athletes and business people come into your country. Jamaica is under quarantine not by man but by God – Good God himself.

To the travel agencies that say you cannot refund people's money because they will now cancel their bookings with you, duly refund the money owed to people because they are following the orders of God – Good God and not the orders of man. You stiff the people of their refund, I am truly hoping Good God leaves you and your family homeless and penniless not just on earth but in hell as well as his abode. No you cannot get into his abode because you will be locked out.

If you cannot refund these people their money then suggest Cuba, Costa Rico, Grand Cayman, South Africa, Seychelles, Martinique, St. Kitts and Nevis to name a few. Good God did not deem these lands unclean. He only deemed Jamaica unclean so rebook to another tropical destination if you have to or can.

Like I said, there is a physical death and a spiritual death with spiritual death being the harshest death anyone can face.

The death of flesh is just the death of flesh but the death of spirit is the final death – the death of you – the true you.

Goodness cannot die but all sins must die and do die.

You have to know your goodness and you have to know Good God. If you don't then you are doomed.

You cannot say someone died for you because this is wrong. You cannot take the story of Jesus to Good God because God – Good God infinitely and indefinitely do not deal in death contrary to what you read in these books sometimes. I too have to get God – Good God to think and see things from my standpoint not my way. Yes he's the higher authority but I too have to question his validity with what's happening in on earth. We need the truth and if he's not giving it – the truth then something is infinitely wrong.

Michelle Jean

God – Good God have mercy upon my soul because the time of man – humanity is now winding down.

Many will be jobless
Homeless

Many will fall ill to greater sickness and diseases because the earth will stop yielding her goodness to humanity – wicked and evil people.

1313 draws to a close and I've yet to receive your true glory – your financial prosperity.

Good God I've done what you've required of me hence stand firmly and truthfully with me and let us save our people.

God – Good God I know your time is not the time of man but I truly need you to guide me always so that I do not slip and fall.

The will of evil is strong, but truly let the will of good – your good will be stronger than that of evil from now on.

Lovey we cannot afford to fail.
We have to do right by our people.
We have to truly save them and be rid of evil forevermore.

Please do not fail me now because I truly need to be in the womb of life – South Africa.

God – Good God, I have to look to you for all this because I truly do not want or need the devil's own. I need your own which is the goodness of You and Mother Earth.

Good God we cannot fail Mother Earth either because she too is depending on you like me.

I truly need your goodness Good God so please bless me with your goodness, your good financial prosperity, your true love, your honesty, the financial prosperity of all of Mother Earth, the trees and water including good food of Mother Earth, the good and true people of Mother Earth and your abode. Good God I need this so I can help clean up land, people and Mother Earth because her trees, her waterways and land need cleaning as well.

Continue to bless Mother Earth as well as keep her safe from wicked and evil people.

Michelle Jean
December 15, 2013

Good God on my birthday please declare the glory of earth and myself in goodness and in truth because I need goodness in my life right now.

Truly bless the earth and me with your goodness all around. Good God I cannot think of me alone I have to think of earth as well as you.

Good God bless you as well on my birthday and come dine with me because I need 2014 and beyond to be our rising of Goodness and Truth – Financial Prosperity and Wealth.

Good God I so do not want or need you to be stingy with me. I need all your goodness abundantly.

Good God we need to do something positive now and it starts with you and me. I truly need you because I know of the womb hence I truly need to be in the cradle of life with you. Hey we need to be each other's protector all around in a good way. I also need Mother Earth to protect me as well hence we need to bond truthfully and honestly with her because she is a part of you. She is a part of good life.

We cannot ignore her because she did not pollute herself. Man – humanity polluted her without caring about her life and well being.

Good God you know me and technology – how I loathe and despise it. You have no privacy with technology hence I need to go back to nature. I need to walk and talk in goodness and in truth with nature.

So Good God truly take me out of the lion's den of man and let me come and live with you.

I need your strength and goodness.

I need Earth's strength and goodness. So please let us bond together with you in a good and true way.

Michelle Jean
December 15, 2013

The life I know is not the life you know

The life I see is not the life you see

In all I see I see death
I see the death of man – humanity

I see fighting
I see hatred
The ills of man – humanity

I see killing

I see people

I see the rise of death

The fall of man
Lands
Humanity

In all I see death
The death of man
The extinction of humanity

Michelle Jean
December 20, 2013

Man it's been a crazy life

24 000 years is almost up
The harvest comes
Woe be unto man

In all that man do, they pay to die because no
one can pay to live.

The seasons come now
They change
The lava rises
Will heat up the lands of earth

Water shortage
Food shortage
Hence the harvest comes

We did want death hence we sinned for death –
to die.

Praise be unto the Lord.
Death comes and every human that has and
have drank the blood of sorrow – the lamb and
death must pay. They must surely die because
death comes to collect his massive pay. And that
pay is the souls – spirit of every sinful human.

Michelle Jean
December 20, 2013

Yes I am at the end of this book and I am so not into it. I couldn't care less for some reason because nothing is going right for me.

2014 comes and I couldn't care less what happens to man hence this dream.

I dreamt (December 21, 2013) Drake the rapper committed suicide and this other rapper Drizzy something got shot – murdered. In the dream I knew the name but when I woke up I truly forgot the next person's name.

In the dream I was a spectator hence I do not put any merit to this dream at all but I am telling you anyway. This is like the Tina Turner dream only she got married and did not die.

So with me seeing the death of Drake, I saw him with this young black lady and it was as if they were at his prom – a prom because they were nicely dressed. This was what the news cast was showing. Suffice it to say I was not into his death. The news cast was saying it was a coincidence with them the news cast stretching out coincidence that he Drake and this other rapper died. They basically died at the same time. Coincidence was spelt coincidenceeeeeeeeeeeeee. Like I said they stretched the word out.

With the death of Drake people was lined up for miles to show their respect and you could see the pretty flowers. The news showed inside of Drakes home and at the top of the stairs I saw this apparition. It come in like dem movie ghost with the bright light but you could not see her face. But the apparition was a lady. The camera did not pick her up because as the camera panned up to view the upstairs she hid but I saw her. There was also this white man dressed in black. He reminded me of those ancient vampires that wore black. He was levitating up from the ground floor and moving up in the air.

That was Drake's part of the dream.

Keep in mind it's a all in one dream.

After seeing this, I saw the next person that died. It's like he was coming out of a restaurant or hotel and as soon as he stepped out someone pulled a gun and shot him in the abdomen – stomach and he died. I did not see the person that shot him all I saw was the gun. Like I said, I was not penetrating the dream because when it was announced that Drake committed suicide, I said to myself in the dream and in the living who the hell cares. I honestly did not give if shit if he died.

In truth too I was reminded of Michael Jackson in the dream and how he killed himself so it mattered not if Drake did the same thing.

I know it's weird and you might be saying how heartless I am on this day but I truly do not care. Seen too much death in 2013 hence this book is ending with death.

Also, to the Duncan Family – the family of Michael Clarke Duncan. Settle your damned affairs because I do not want to see Michael again. This is the second time I am seeing this man and your family is stressing him out.

He never had gray in his face and now he's getting gray because of your nastiness.

He's not a nasty man because I saw him in green. If you go to Google images and type in the colour green you will see the green he was in. Look for Background it's the last image in the first row of images. The light that emulates the green is the colour green he was in. And for all of you out there that is what the colour of my tree of life looks like, hence I call it Tomato Green.

Like I said, he was dressed in this colour hence do right by him and give him his headstone. DO NOT DICK AROUND WITH HIM IN DEATH because from the looks of it, he was not dirty he was clean and you are the ones to be stressing him out in death and wanting to make him unclean. So settle your differences because if I see him again, I and he speaks to me, I will tell him to make all of you lose it all. And do not say I can't because none of you know the spiritual world like I do. Give him his rights and let him be free to live stress free.

In the dream he was with 2 other gentleman. He was in the middle and he was smiling at me. Man he has a beautiful smile hence I can't believe he's dead. His death along with Paul Walker's death was hot. I felt those two deaths but none of you would know about death's sting if you know not death.

Wow. I am going to leave it at that.

Like I said, Michael was with two other gentleman and he had gray fuzzy on his face. One man asked me about an apartment and I told him I know nothing about it but if he went to the superintendent he would be able to tell him about the apartment. He was also in green but on his suit – green suit, he had a smudge on it. Meaning he was not clean hence someone in the Duncan family is not clean. Something is wrong somewhere, so I am telling you to fix the problem and stop the damned bickering. It's amazing how we care not for our loved ones in the living but as soon as dem dead wi fight ova wey ano fiwi. Wi fight ova dead lef.

Bunch of gold diggers that rob the dead of his rights.

Fix the head stone issue and stop bickering over his dead lef because like I said, if I see him again I will tell him to make all of you lose every penny including apartment – home. And no, I will not use bad words because I know who the damned gold digger is. The unclean beast so truly get your priorities straight and give him rest.

Di man wuk so damn hard inna life fi unnu a cheat him in death like a unnu wuk fi it. Damn greedy but trust me the grave is waiting for the lots of you.

Yes I am mad because none of you truly knew his gentle spirit.

None of you knew his smile.

That smile is so beautiful that when you see it it brings peace to your soul.

Please let him continue to smile hence give him rest come on now.

How would any of you like it if someone was stressing you out in death?

Yu si if he was a Jamaican Duppy none a unnu would a sleep because him oulda mek unnu faate.

Yu noa hoo much rock stone woulda fling pan unnu house top.

Yu noa hoo much bulb woulda blow infront a unnu face.

Yu noa hoo much fiya woulda bun inna unnu house.

Truss mi unnu lucky him no meet up on di right Jamaican duppy dem. Because if he did, not one of you would have any peace in your home.

Truss mi unnu woulda si bush a bun an sey a God a di burning bush like in the time of Moses of your book of sin.

Fiya woulda blaze inna unna ass yu si. Das why we noa bout burning bush and rolling calf – the cow wey come with fiya. Some a unnu need demya kine of blazing and backsiding. And yes some of this dream is for me too hence the book a little advice – talk.

Yes I had to get that book in before today and I did that.

I know I am jumping ahead but it cannot be helped hence below.

Michelle Jean
December 21 & 25, 2013

It's December 25, 2013 early morning and I cannot go back to sleep.

2013 Wow.

I uploaded A Little Advice – Talk on Lulu December 24, 2013. For some strange reason I had to finish up that book and upload it before the 25th and I did.

Wow when it comes to that book because I went off and I guess death never took too kindly to me cursing him and his family.

Yes people Death found me.

Trust me I've never seen this type of death before. I've told you evil dead die as a White Person dressed in White and it matters not what colour you are; this how wicked people die in the spiritual realm.

This morning I dreamt I went someplace but I am not sure if it was Africa.

This Black African King dressed in full White Islamic attire approached me. He gave a glass of water with ice floating at the top. The water had a little bit of cloud in it but I did not put anything to it. But I noticed the little bit of cloud anyway. You know when you turn your pipe on and run it but a little yiddy bit of Chlorine is left in the water. That's the cloudiness I am talking about.

This Black King fed me the water himself. It's was like wow a Black King feeding me. Well the fed he fed me the water, he kept the glass of ice water to my head and people I could not breathe. He was killing me. I managed to wake up out of my sleep and when I did go back to sleep the same thing happened again. I am getting water by this king and dying in the process of drinking the water. I woke up again and here I am editing this book and telling you about my dream.

And no people this was not one of those dreams where someone is holding you down and you can't scream out. I was literally dying – could not breathe.

And no for you who are going to say it's sleep apnea.

Like I've told you, death wants me because I am a treat to death and his people.

I was told to write a book by Good God and I told him Good God that I will not write lies and I refuse to write lies.

What I dream as well as see before me I let you know. ***Humanity need to know the true truth hence the truth is death to sin and death.***

Humanity must not know the truth with them because if you know the full truth – the truth many of you will leave his fold and he death cannot afford to lose one individual.

Yes I cursed Sin and Death including the parents of Sin and Death and I make no apologies to any of them for what I've done.

Sin has no right to cause anyone to sin hence sin and death must come to an end.

Death must collect his pay and that is his wicked and sinful people – evil and wicked people and truly leave the planet earth.

Hence I will forever ask God – Good God, when did loving us so become hating us so?

When did loving us so become aiding the devil – death in killing his good and true people?

When did loving us so become the death of your messengers – children by the hands of death?

When did loving me so become the death of me?

Family – my true family. Usually white for me in a dream is good. This is the first time it has been associated with death – my death.

Trust me I cannot comprehend this because this is a Black King too.

I told you about the different black hue in the spiritual realm. This Black King was black but not as black as that black hue.

This King was Muslim because he wore Islamic garb. Wow.

Wow

Wow because I truly do not know what to say but it matters not to me. I am trying not to swear but I am going to anyway.

Fuck the Islamic Kingdoms and their king of death because I truly do not fear death and what they want to do unto me.

I KNOW THAT ISLAM IS A SPIRITUAL PRISON IN THE SPIRITUAL WORLD HENCE CURSE BE UNTO THEM INFINITELY AND INDEFINITELY FOR TIME TIMES TIME AND BEYOND FOREVER EVER INDEFINITELY.

Islam is a fucking curse to all of humanity because the devil uses Islam to trap the souls – spirit of black people in hell hence there is no escape for many of them.

Many of these Black Imam's tell you to change your name to Mohammed – the son of death hence many of you have done this. Changed your names to death hence you're all fucking hell bound.

You have your DDC because many of you were not born Mohammed or Ali or whatever name the devil tell you to change your name to.

Many of you were born:
Johnson
Jones
Smith
Williams
Thomas
Brown
Wilkins
Jenkins and so forth. And when you change your name to reflect the Islamic names of the dead, you are going against Good God himself.

MEANING YOU CHANGED YOUR NAME TO REFLECT A LIE. YOU ALSO GIVE YOUR CHILDREN THE NAME AND

NAMES OF DEATH SO THEY TOO MUST BE IMPRISONED AND ENSLAVED IN HELL FOR THIS LIE.

HENCE MAKING YOU AN INFINITE AND INDEFININTE LIAR – SINNER IN THE EYES AND SIGHT OF GOOD GOD.

Yes Islam once belonged to us but because it became polluted – dirty, it no longer became of us. Hence we are infinitely and indefinitely not allowed to practice the Islamic Way.

That way is no longer of peace hence Islam is condemned by God – Good God. It is now a lie meaning it's about religious lies that teach wrong.

Death, the death of all is their motto because if you are not of Islam – the sacrificial lamb of death you are wrong in their eyes.

LIES ARE WRONG AND ISLAM IS WRONG INFINITELY AND INDEFINITELY. Hence I've told you it is not baane yah Muslims that get the life line in the grave it's the converted ones.

And I know it's not all converted ones that get this life line.

Many of you that have and has given your children the name of Mohammed when they should have been given the name Johnson or McCloud have and has condemned your child to death.

YOU HAVE INFINITELY AND INDEFINITELY GIVEN THEM THEIR DDC – Death's Death Certificate.

You as a parent made your child and or children wrong in the eyes and sight of Good God, hence the condemnation to hell by you as a parent.

Your child is going to die there are no ands ifs or buts about this. Thus saith the Lord thy God meaning it is so. You are also going to die because you committed a grave sin – wrong.

No one can change his or her birth certificate because none can change their death certificate.

Like I said and will forever tell you. Good God gave us good life and we are the ones to give it up, throw it away for death.

The lie for many is sweet but in the end it's bitter to the stomach.

So to you the Islamic King or Black King of Death curse be unto you infinitely and indefinitely forever ever for what you tried to do to me.

Infinite and indefinite curse be unto the every Islamic kingdom of earth, the spiritual realm and beyond.

Curse upon curses be unto the people.

Curse upon curses be unto every land.

Curse upon curses infinitely and indefinitely for more than infinite and indefinite lifetimes to come. So to you King damn you unto hell as well as curse of curses be unto you in hell and in hell fire.

I do not play games and right now I am truly fed up of sin and death and his evil and wicked people in the living and the spiritual realm.

Like I said, I do not bother you leave me alone because I do get stinker than sin and I do condemn all around. Do not anger me hence none of you will like it now.

Islam is an infinite lie hence it's condemned. Islam is what the devil uses to convert and condemn Black People to death – hell.

Religion is an infinite lie hence religion – all forms of religion is condemned. Religion kills not only the flesh but the soul – spirit.

Listen, I've come too far to let this Muslim Man – King of death rock me. Hence curse him and Islam as well as all Islamic Kingdom infinitely and indefinitely on this day, December 25, 2013.

Burn in hell because death is not my home or stay, life – good life is, hence Good God is in the midst of all that I do.

Remember no Babylonian is on the Mountain of Good God so what say any of you?

Your lies are done because I know the lie.

I know the lies of religion.

I know the lies and deceit of you hence God – Good God does not deal in religion only death do, hence you tell humanity to kill – die.

You tell your people when you kill you go straight to paradise

to see Allah. BUT I SAY UNTO YOU. YOU ARE A LIAR AND A DECEIVER BECAUSE WHEN YOU KILL YOU DIE TO SEE DEATH. HENCE YOU GO TO HELL AND BURN. YOU GO TO HELL TO TASTE THE FIRES OF HELL BEFORE YOUR EVENTUAL DEATH.

Hence, "the wages of sin is death and thou shalt not kill."

Anyone that willing kills – take the flesh of another human being must face hell – go to hell and die. Hence God – Good God does not deal with lies and deceit nor does he deal with or look upon the children of sin and death because nothing truthful comes from your lips – mouth only lies and deceit.

You all claim Islam is the truth but Islam is a lie because many of you live to kill then spread lies and say you are going to see Allah.

First of all comprehend this.

Allah is taken from the root word Allelujah and Allah means the BREATH OF LIFE.

Islam – you the people of Islam otherwise called MUSLIMS kill the BREATH OF LIFE. So when you kill the Breath of Life here on earth with your lies and killing, how are you going to see Allah? You take life hence you are of the walking and living dead.

Yes I have condemned you and cursed you because none of you hath life – true life. You all have death. You're all apart of death – the dead.

None of you have the Breath of Life because none of you, not one of you know what the Breath of Life is.

Moses knew hence he took life out of Egypt and brought it into a land where it would be safe until the appointed time – the death of sin hence the death of death.

Take a good look at the Ying and Yang and you will see Life – the Breath of Life which is life itself.

Ya'll want it but can't have because as Bob Marley eloquently put it in Time Will Tell, Jah would never give the power to a bald head. And like I've said before, you're all bald heads.

You're all wannabes.

Wannabe Jews but infinitely and indefinitely cannot be because you're all the true children of the dead – Satan himself.

Yes the true spawn of Satan and Eve.

Yes, No Weapon by Fred Hammond has been my anthem for 2013 and as I close this book, I dedicate No Weapon infinitely and indefinitely to Good God's children – people.

No weapon (s) formed against us shall prosper because he Good God is with us.

He's in the midst of us.
He surrounds us.

He truly loves us.

So to every Islamic country that kill for sport and lie to its people including humanity, truly curse be unto you infinitely and indefinitely because none of you are of Life – Good God nor are any of you of the Breath of Life because you all take life.

You're all evil – condemned hence you slaughter and kill to go to hell.

You truly take life without remorse then turn around and LIE ON THE BREATH OF LIFE.

Allelujah.

Praise be unto you Good God because the truth must come out and now the devil and his people will truly have hell to pay.

Now you can finally wash me clean because this aspect of my job and journey is done. I've truly handed the devil – death back his people because they are so not wanted in the life of all that is good and true including the earth.

Like I said, the truth must be known and I am infinitely fed up of wicked and evil people that live to kill and destroy. You created all that is good and it is not right for sin and his evil set of people to come and destroy you and all the goodness you have given to humanity.

Hence I hand you back goodness and truth Good God so that you can live in goodness and truth with your people infinitely and indefinitely forever ever.

You need to be in the midst of our goodness and truth and if this is the way to do it. Hand you back your goodness and truth then I make no apologies unto anyone. Enough is enough.

Like I've said, you do not lock anyone out of your good and true kingdom – abode. We are the ones to.

Your prerequisite has always been truth, honesty and cleanliness. Goodness hence nothing has or have change over the course of history.

Yes I am angry but take your victory because if I had to do this again, I would not hesitate to curse Sin and his Family.

And anyone that say I have no right to do what I did. Truly think about Good God, the Earth and all the innocent lives that have been taken by the hands of wicked and evil people over the course of history.

Like I said, Good God does not lock anyone out of his kingdom hence the curse can be redeemed. I am not judge, jury nor am I the executioner. I am fed up of what sin and his people are doing to humanity hence I've exercised my right as a child of God – Good God when it comes to the wages of sin is death law or clause.

Sin wants to destroy it all and kill all and I am saying you can't because, "the wages of sin is death and thou shalt not kill." And no I did not kill anyone I just cursed them. Death has his keep. Now the law and laws of Sin must be carried out. As for the curse that was put on you the White Race, I leave that in Good God's capable hands. Hopefully the curse will be lifted so that you don't have to fight and kill so much because like I said, I did see one White on the mountain of Good God. Some of you I know cannot be saved nor do I want to save some of you. Too damned racist and wicked but to curse you is another.

Know that I did not curse these people for cursing sake. I am just fed up of the evils that they do. Now the shoe is on the other foot now let's see how sin an evil like it in the physical and spiritual realm. Hence I hand Good God and the Earth the victory as well as all that is good back to them infinitely and indefinitely forever ever. This new seal of goodness cannot be broken hence all evil must leave earth infinitely and indefinitely. We need truth and peace now and it's time for Goodness to live in true peace and harmony forever ever.

Who has their DDC cannot be saved because they gave death their souls or spirit anyway.

Who has their DC can be saved hence they must now walk and live clean and good – true.

Truth and cleanliness is a prerequisite hence the killing of the Breath of Life must stop.

The lies told on the Breath of Life must stop.

The lies told on Good God himself must stop.

The religious hatred must stop.

The converting and condemning humanity to hell must stop.

YOU WANT TO SEE GOD – GOOD GOD THEN DO RIGHT BY SELF AND HIM GOOD GOD. COME ON NOW.

You cannot live your life in lies and expect all to be well with God come on now.

Truth is the key to life and without it you are dead, like unto the living breathing and walking dead.

Yes every man has a right to live but when evil and sin, wicked and evil people continuously hurt others I draw the line.

As human beings we need to do better and not let religious lies govern our lives.

I do not like sin or death hence they are condemned.

I will not interfere with sins people but when sin – death interfere with me then we have a problem.

Are my hands still clean?

I will let you know. Just know that I cannot curse good nor will I ever curse good. You can only curse evil.

Michelle Jean
December 25, 2013

OTHER BOOKS BY MICHELLE JEAN

Blackman Redemption – The Fall of Michelle Jean
Blackman Redemption – After the Fall Apology
Blackman Redemption – World Cry – Christine Lewis
Blackman Redemption
Blackman Redemption – The Rise and Fall of Jamaica
Blackman Redemption – The War of Israel
Blackman Redemption – The Way I Speak to God
Blackman Redemption – A Little Talk With Man
Blackman Redemption – The Den of Thieves
Blackman Redemption – The Death of Jamaica
Blackman Redemption – Happy Mother's Day
Blackman Redemption – The Death of Faith
Blackman Redemption – The War of Religion
Blackman Redemption – The Death of Russia
Blackman Redemption – The Truth
Blackman Redemption – Spiritual War

The New Book of Life
The New Book of Life – A Cry For The Children
The New Book of Life – Judgement
The New Book of Life – Love Bound
The New Book of Life - Me

Just One of Those Days
Book Two – Just One of Those Days
Just One of Those Days – Book Three The Way I Feel
Just One of Those Days – Book Four

The Days I Am Weak
Crazy Thoughts – My Book of Sin
Broken

Ode to Mr. Dean Fraser

A Little Little Talk
A Little Little Talk – Book Two

Prayers
My Collective
A Little Talk/A Time For Fun and Play
Simple Poems
Behind The Scars
Songs of Praise And Love

Love Bound
Love Bound – Book Two

Dedication Unto My Kids
More Talk
Saving America From A Woman's Perspective
My Collective the Other Side of Me
My Collective the Dark Side of Me
A Blessed Day
Lose To Win
My Doubtful Days – Book One

My Little Talk With God
My Little Talk With God – Book Two

A Different Mood and World – Thinking

My Nagging Day
My Nagging Day – Book Two

Friday September 13, 2013

My True Love
It Would Be You
My Day

A Little Advice – Talk